JR. GRAPHIC MONSTER STORIES

GHOSTS!

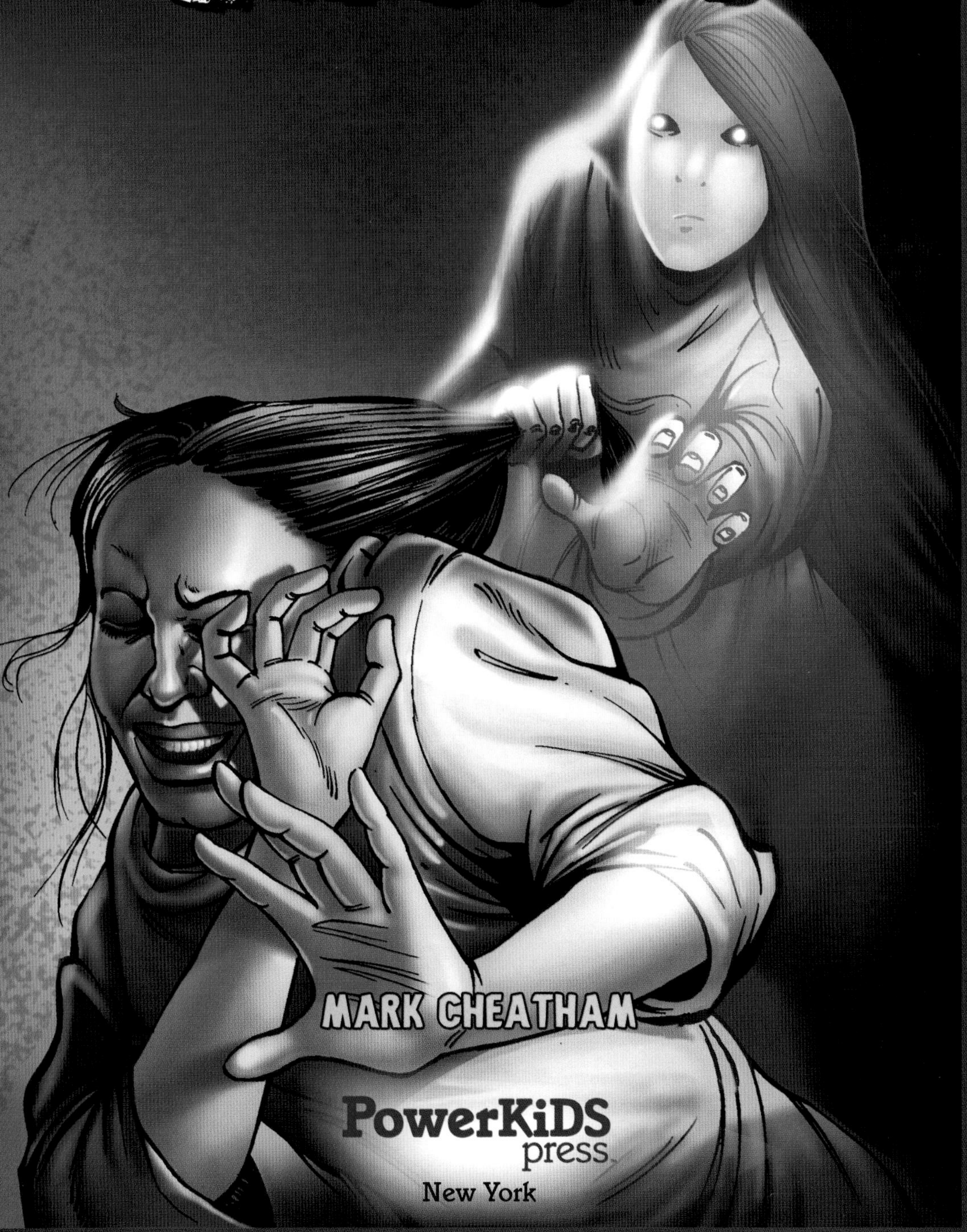

MARK CHEATHAM

PowerKiDS press
New York

Published in 2012 by The Rosen Publishing Group, Inc.

29 East 21st Street, New York, NY 10010

First Edition

Editor: Joanne Randolph
Book Design: Planman Technologies
Illustrations: Planman Technologies

Library of Congress Cataloging-in-Publication Data

Cheatham, Mark.

Ghosts! / by Mark Cheatham. — 1st ed.

   p. cm. — (Jr. graphic monster stories)

Includes index.

ISBN 978-1-4488-6223-8 (library binding) — ISBN 978-1-4488-6405-8 (pbk.) — ISBN 978-1-4488-6406-5 (6-pack)

1. Poltergeists—Tennessee—Robertson County—Comic books, strips, etc. 2. Bell family—Miscellanea—Comic books, strips, etc. 3. Ghosts—United States—Comic books, strips, etc. I. Title.

BF1473.B37C54 2012

133.1—dc23

2011028756

Manufactured in the United States of America

CPSIA Compliance Information: Batch #PLW2102PK: For Further Information contact Rosen Publishing, New York, New York at 1-800-237-9932

Contents

Main Characters

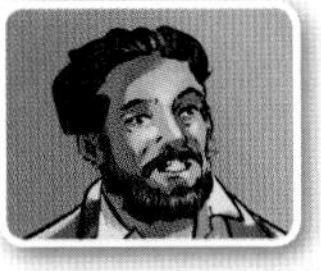

John Bell (1750–1820) Husband of Lucy Bell. He was the main focus of the anger of the ghost of Kate Batts. Some think that the ghost drove John to his death.

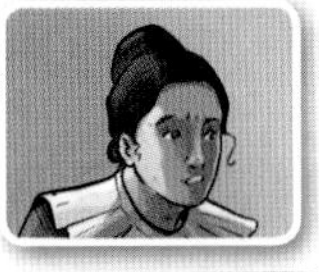

Lucy Bell (1770–1837) Wife of John Bell. She helplessly watched the ghost of Kate Batts abuse her family.

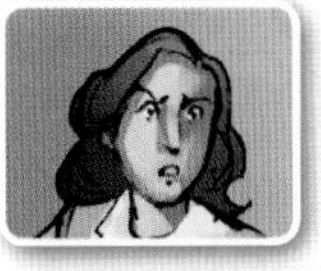

Betsy Bell (1806–1888) Daughter of John and Lucy Bell. She was **tormented** by the ghost of Kate Batts until she broke off her **engagement** to Joshua Gardner.

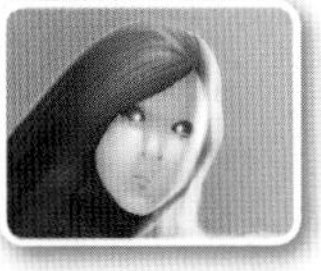

Kate Batts (c. 1700s) **Deceased** neighbor of the Bells who may have believed she was **cheated** by John Bell. Many think that her **spirit** haunted the Bell family for decades.

Ghostly Facts

- **What Is a Ghost?** Those who believe in ghosts think that a person's spirit separates from the body when a person dies. This spirit sometimes continues to live in our world rather than moving on to live in the spirit world. Ghosts usually **haunt** a certain place, such as the home where the ghost lived before death.
- **Getting Rid of a Ghost** Ghost "**experts**" provide guidelines for getting rid of a ghost. Sometimes a ghost will do things in your home such as sing, talk, or make noises. If you have these problems, ask the ghost to stop doing these things. You may also want to ask the ghost simply to leave. Explain to the ghost that it is a spirit and its body is dead. You may need to ask the ghost what it wants. Helping the ghost get what it wants may help it leave. Do not act as if you are afraid.

Ghosts!

CHELSEA AND HER FRIENDS WERE OUT TRICK-OR-TREATING ON HALLOWEEN.

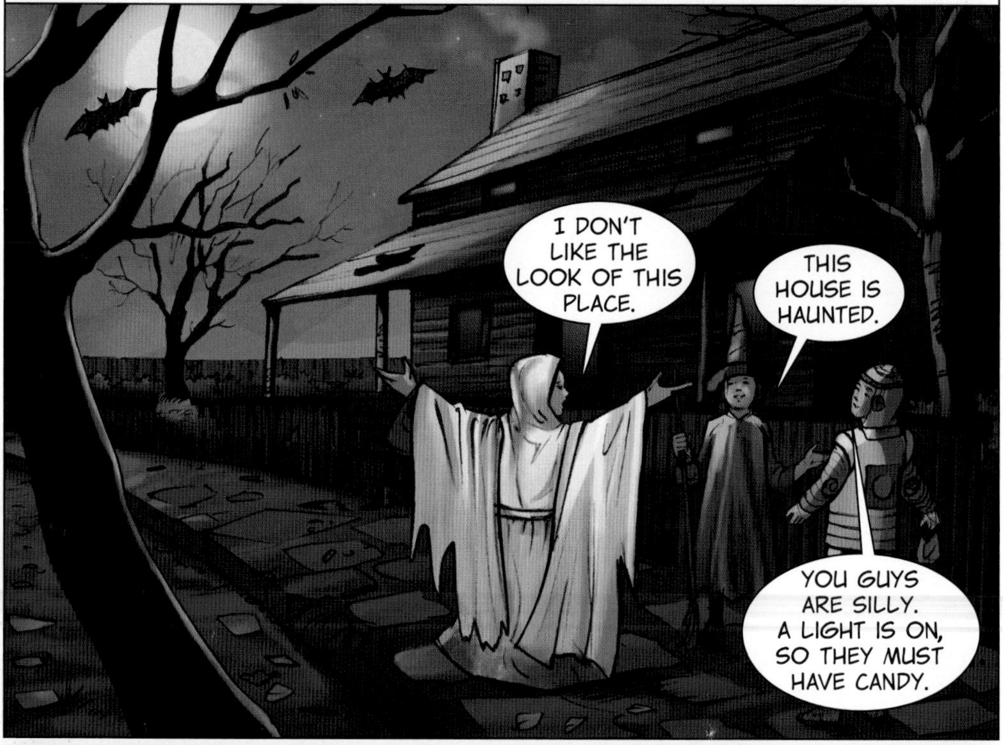
I DON'T LIKE THE LOOK OF THIS PLACE.
THIS HOUSE IS HAUNTED.
YOU GUYS ARE SILLY. A LIGHT IS ON, SO THEY MUST HAVE CANDY.

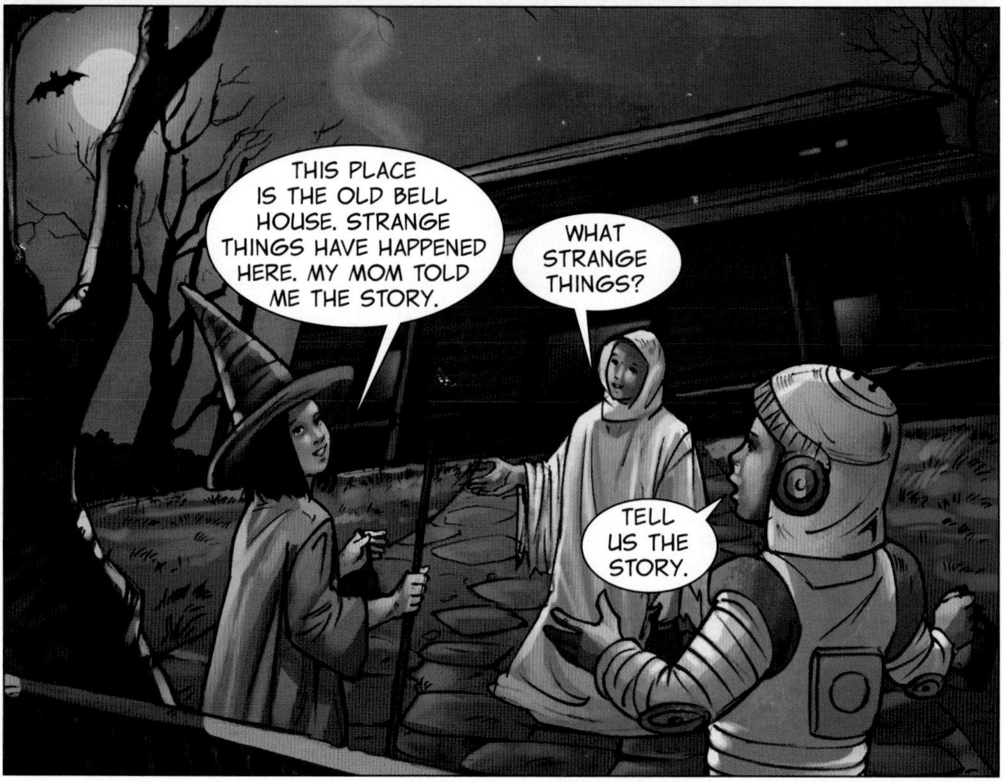
THIS PLACE IS THE OLD BELL HOUSE. STRANGE THINGS HAVE HAPPENED HERE. MY MOM TOLD ME THE STORY.
WHAT STRANGE THINGS?
TELL US THE STORY.

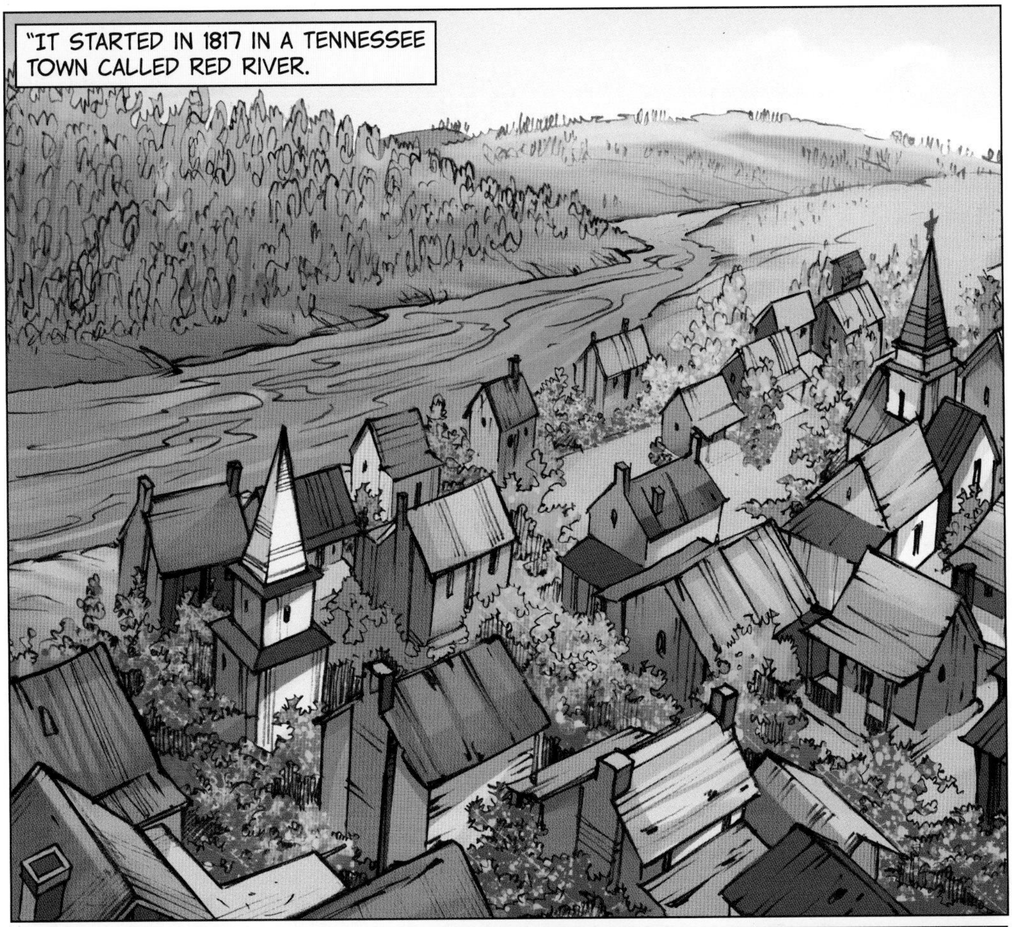
"IT STARTED IN 1817 IN A TENNESSEE TOWN CALLED RED RIVER.

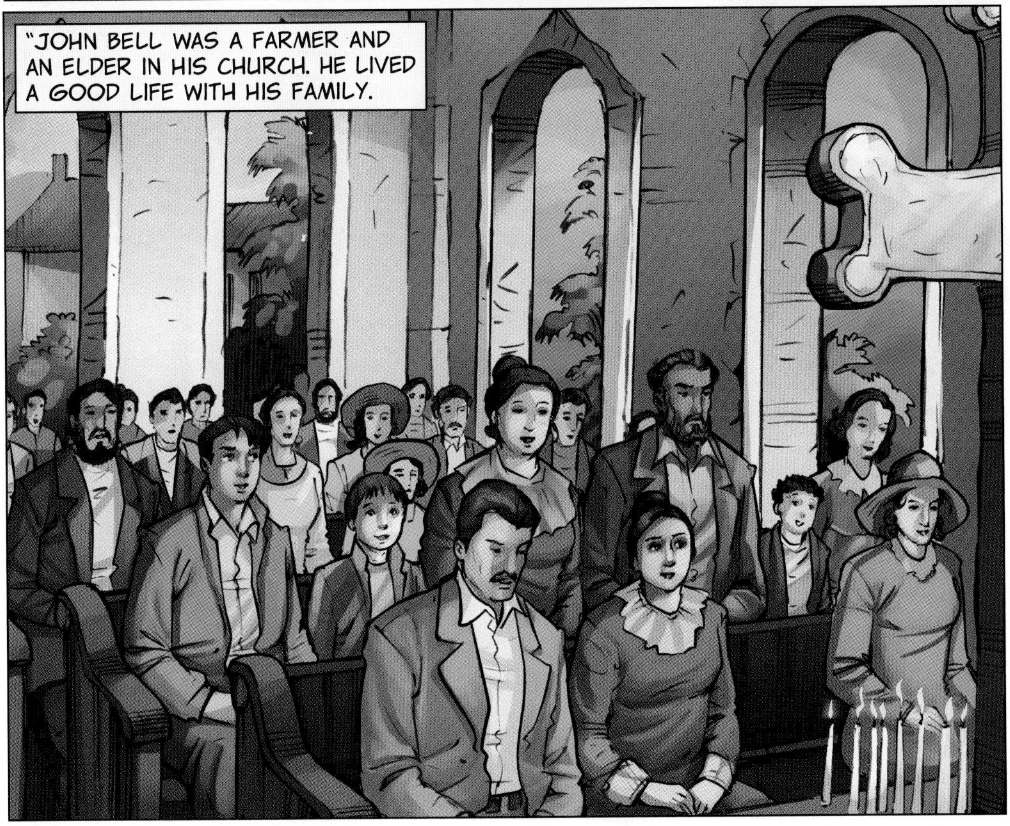
"JOHN BELL WAS A FARMER AND AN ELDER IN HIS CHURCH. HE LIVED A GOOD LIFE WITH HIS FAMILY.

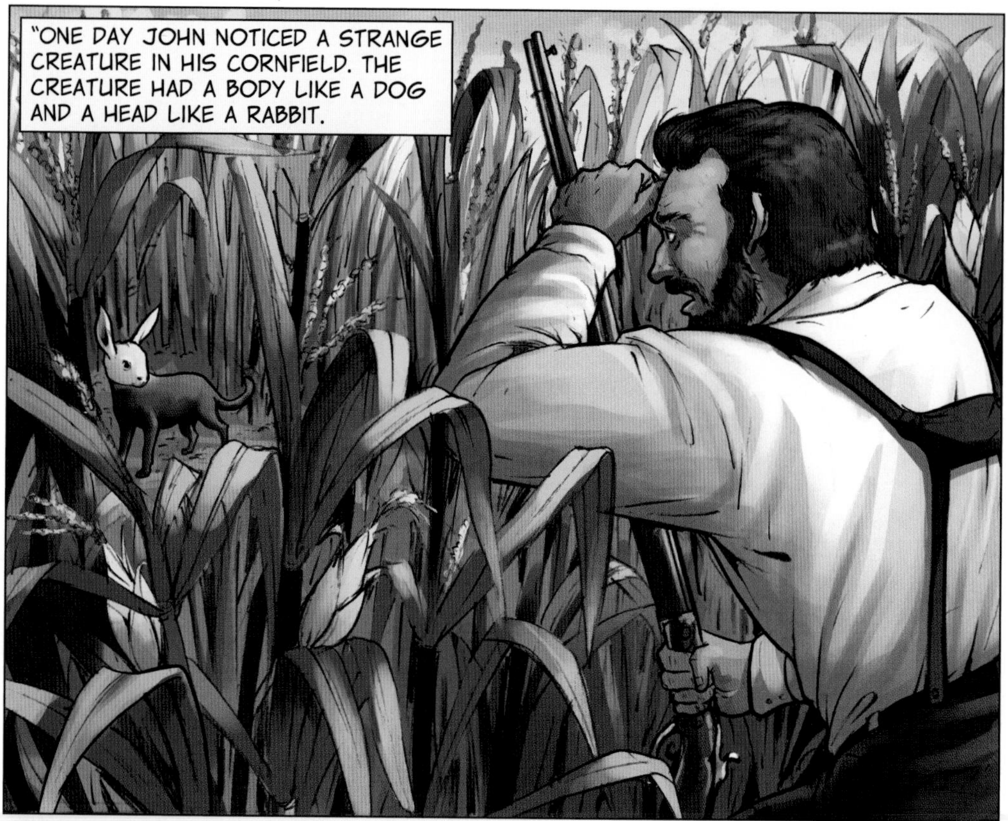
"ONE DAY JOHN NOTICED A STRANGE CREATURE IN HIS CORNFIELD. THE CREATURE HAD A BODY LIKE A DOG AND A HEAD LIKE A RABBIT.

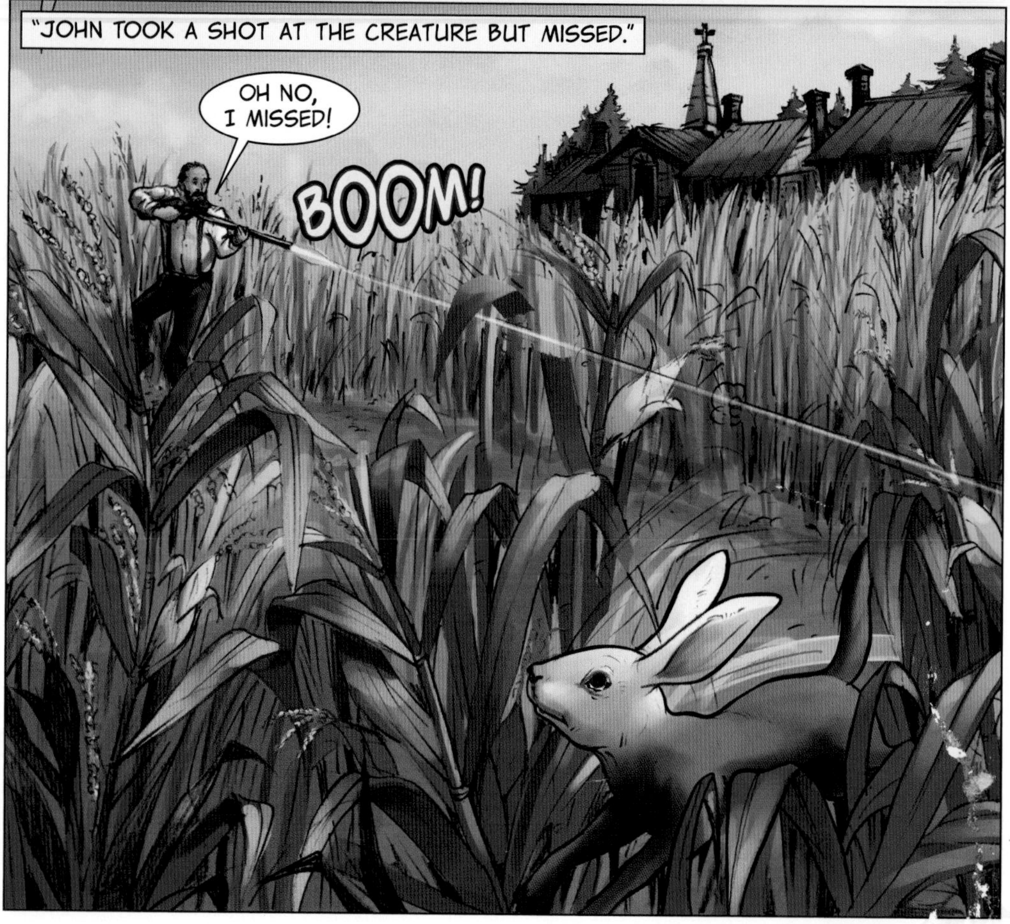
"JOHN TOOK A SHOT AT THE CREATURE BUT MISSED."
OH NO, I MISSED!
BOOM!

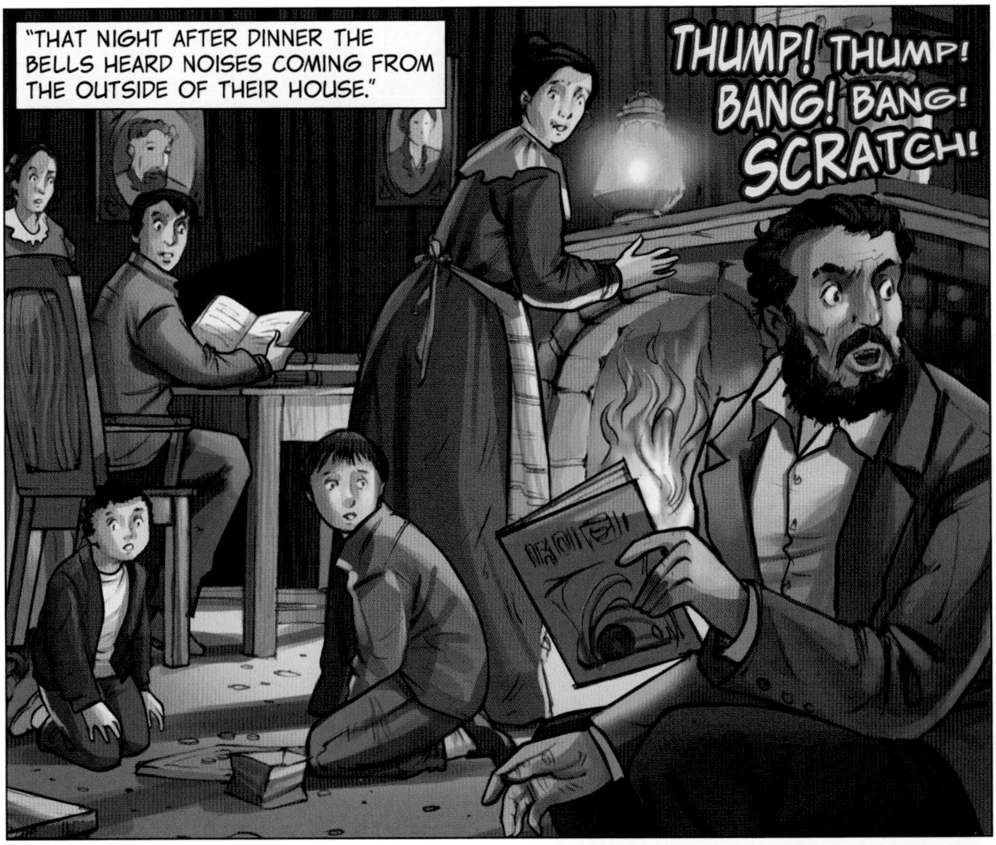
"THAT NIGHT AFTER DINNER THE BELLS HEARD NOISES COMING FROM THE OUTSIDE OF THEIR HOUSE."
THUMP! THUMP!
BANG! BANG!
SCRATCH!

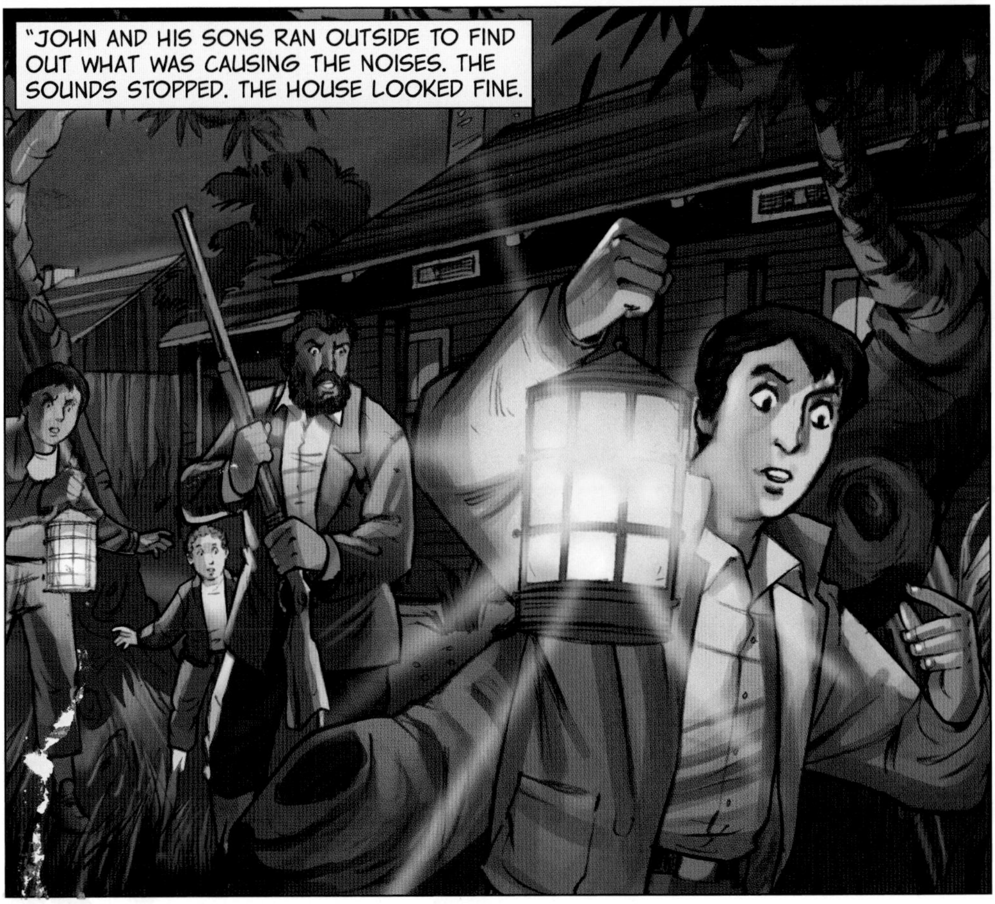
"JOHN AND HIS SONS RAN OUTSIDE TO FIND OUT WHAT WAS CAUSING THE NOISES. THE SOUNDS STOPPED. THE HOUSE LOOKED FINE.

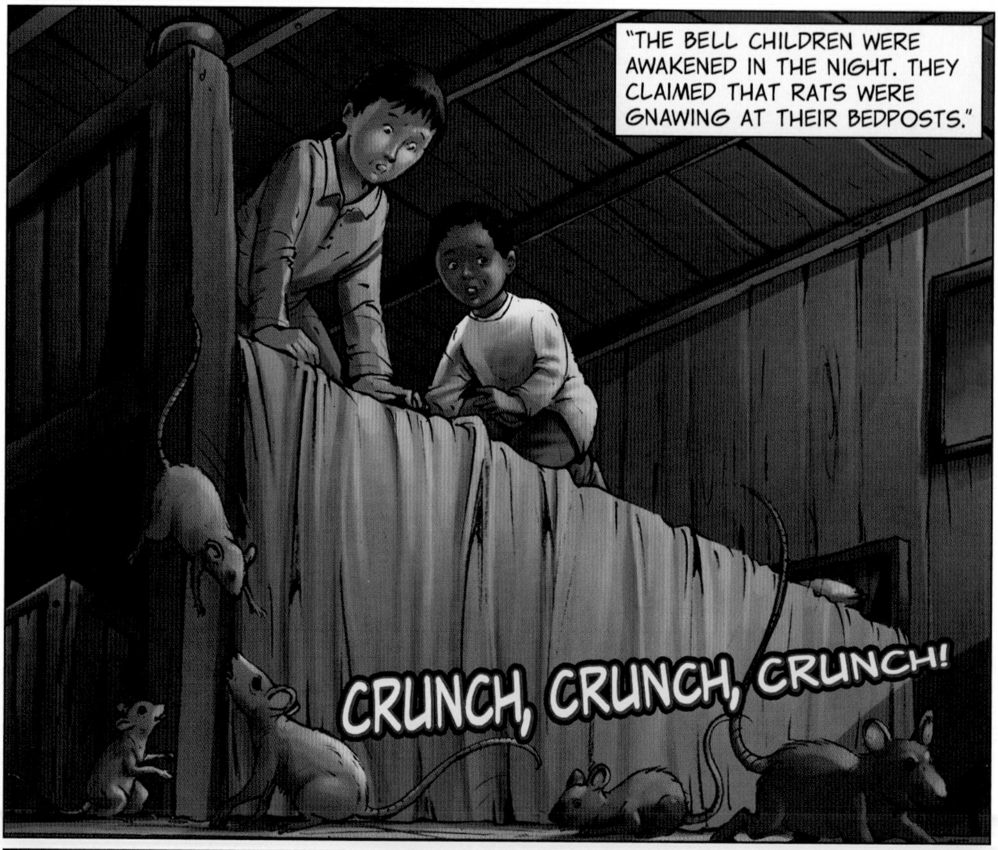
"THE BELL CHILDREN WERE AWAKENED IN THE NIGHT. THEY CLAIMED THAT RATS WERE GNAWING AT THEIR BEDPOSTS."
CRUNCH, CRUNCH, CRUNCH!

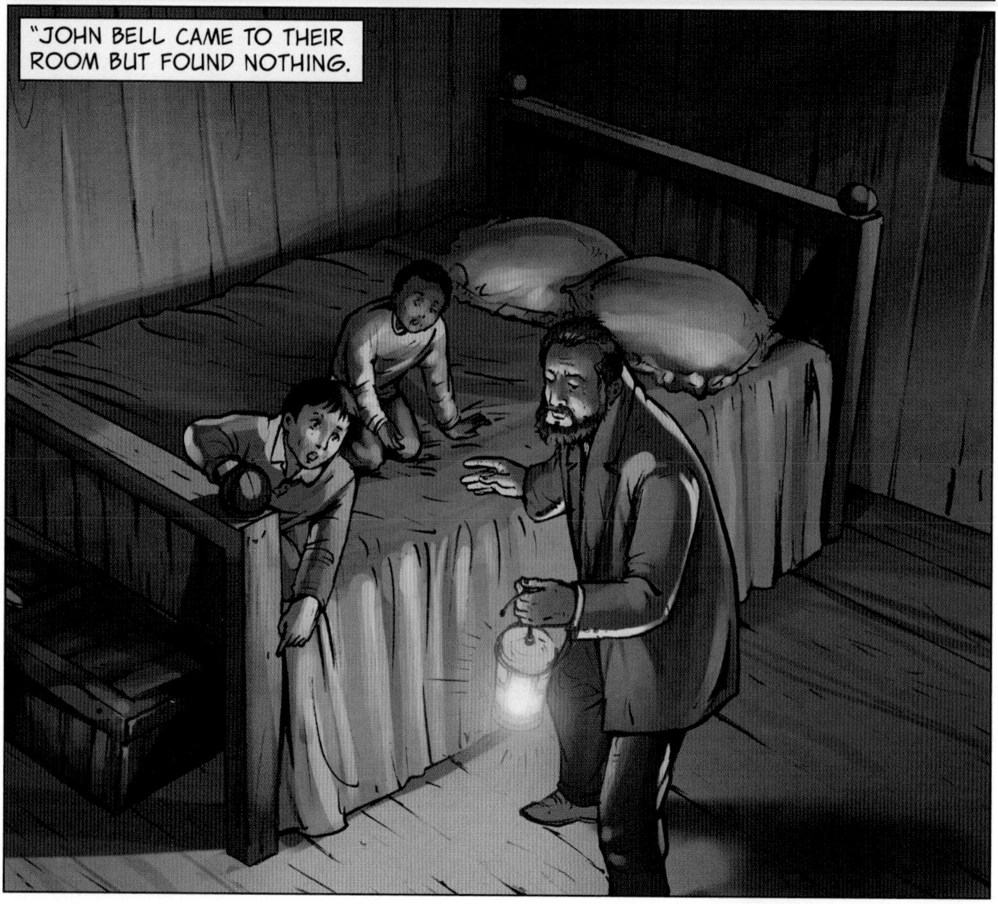
"JOHN BELL CAME TO THEIR ROOM BUT FOUND NOTHING.

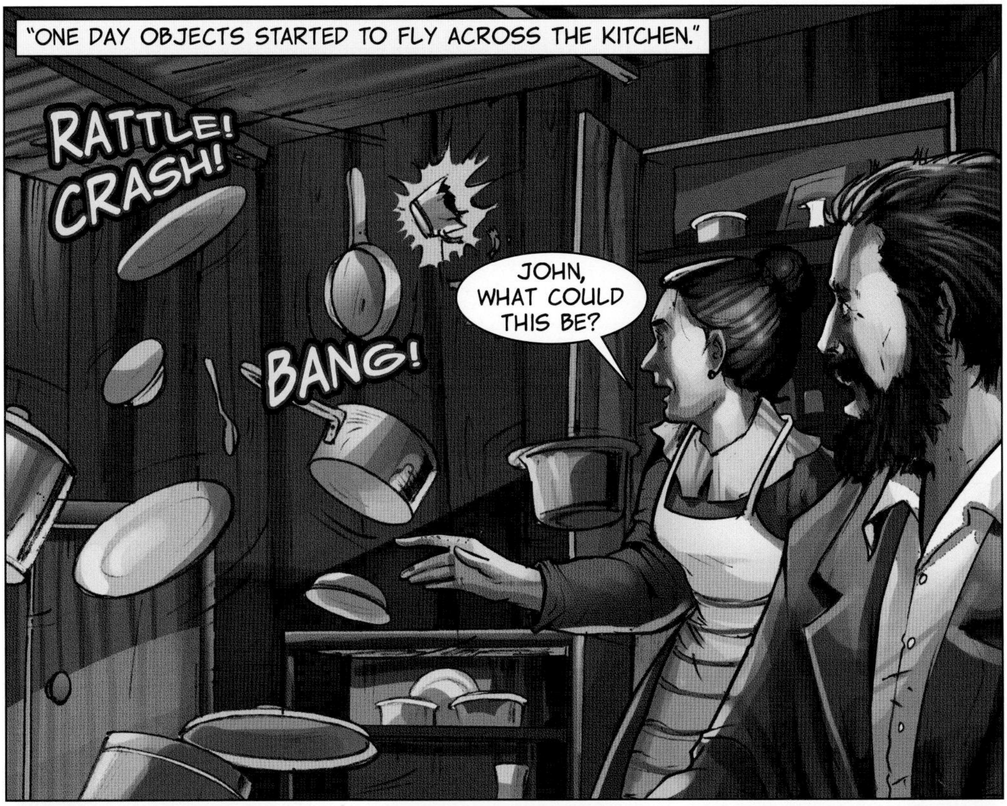
"ONE DAY OBJECTS STARTED TO FLY ACROSS THE KITCHEN."
RATTLE! CRASH!
JOHN, WHAT COULD THIS BE?
BANG!

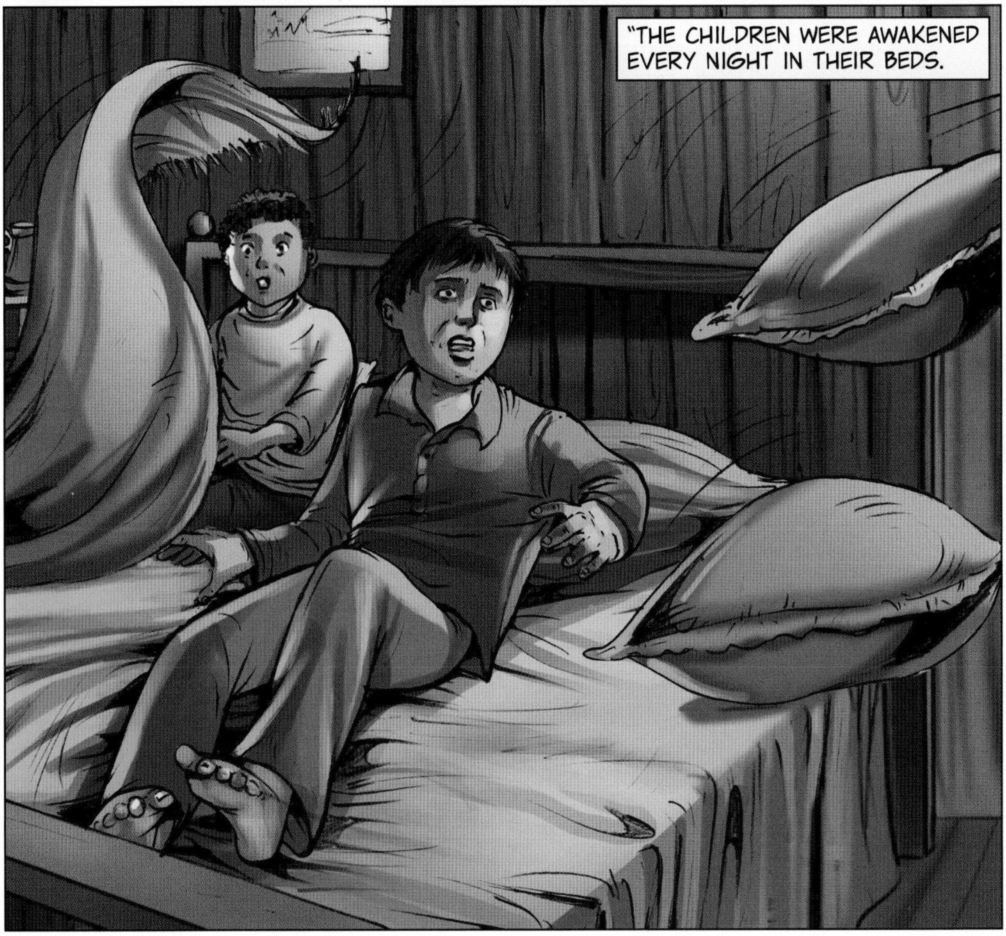
"THE CHILDREN WERE AWAKENED EVERY NIGHT IN THEIR BEDS.

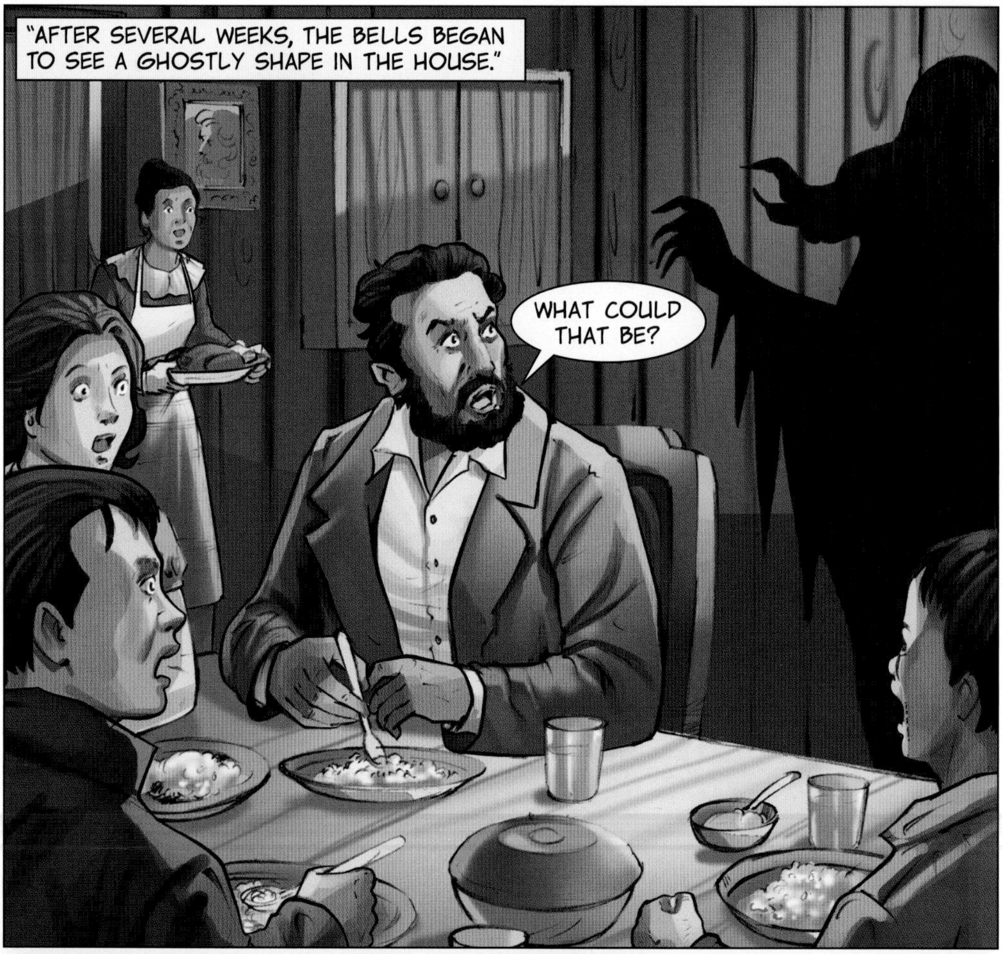
"AFTER SEVERAL WEEKS, THE BELLS BEGAN TO SEE A GHOSTLY SHAPE IN THE HOUSE."
WHAT COULD THAT BE?

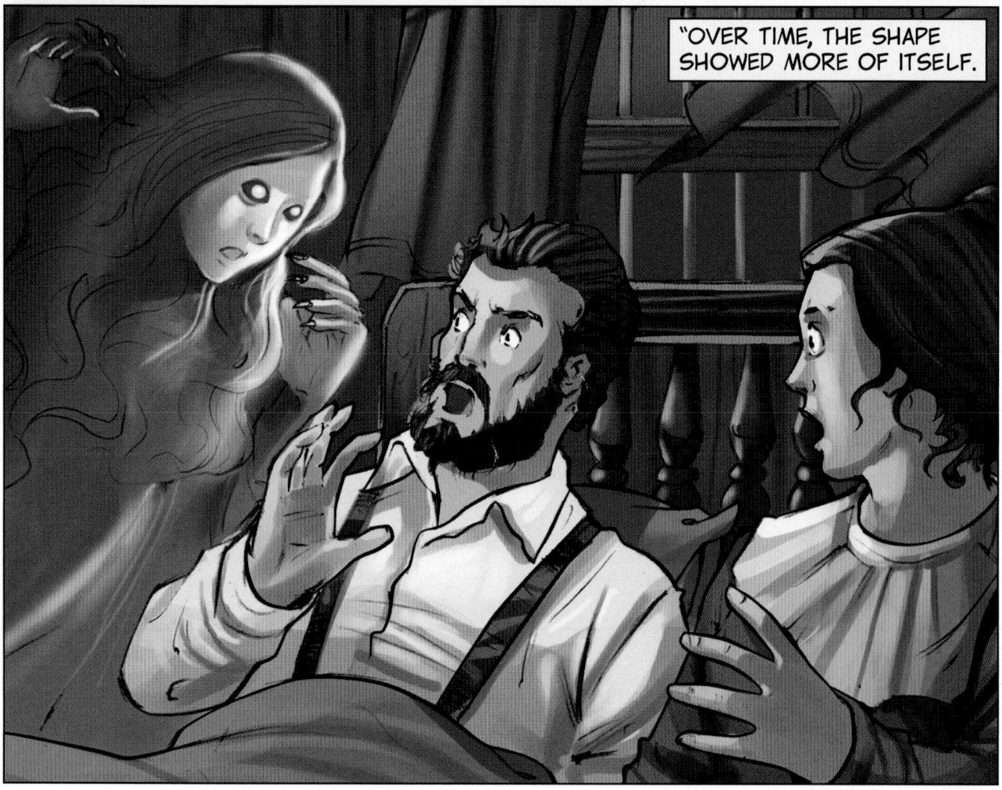
"OVER TIME, THE SHAPE SHOWED MORE OF ITSELF.

"THEN THE GHOST BEGAN TO ATTACK THE BELLS.

"THE GHOST SEEMED TO DISLIKE JOHN BELL IN PARTICULAR."

HA HA HA HA!

I WILL GET YOU, JOHN BELL!

STOP THIS! LEAVE ME ALONE!

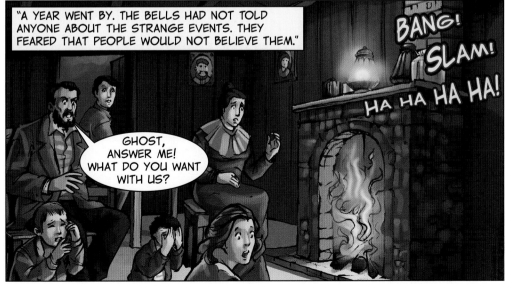

"A YEAR WENT BY. THE BELLS HAD NOT TOLD ANYONE ABOUT THE STRANGE EVENTS. THEY FEARED THAT PEOPLE WOULD NOT BELIEVE THEM."

BANG!
SLAM!
HA HA HA HA!

GHOST, ANSWER ME! WHAT DO YOU WANT WITH US?

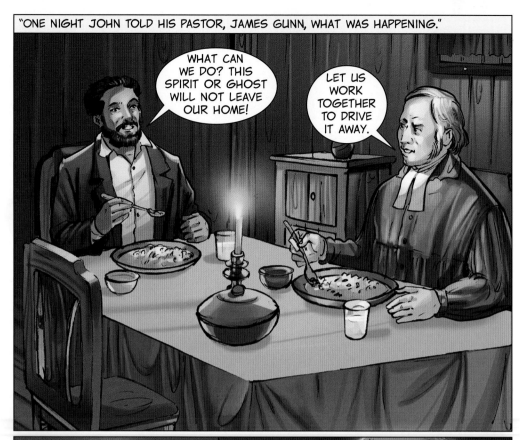

"ONE NIGHT JOHN TOLD HIS PASTOR, JAMES GUNN, WHAT WAS HAPPENING."

WHAT CAN WE DO? THIS SPIRIT OR GHOST WILL NOT LEAVE OUR HOME!

LET US WORK TOGETHER TO DRIVE IT AWAY.

"THE PASTOR SPENT THE NIGHT AT JOHN'S HOUSE AND SAW THE GHOST.

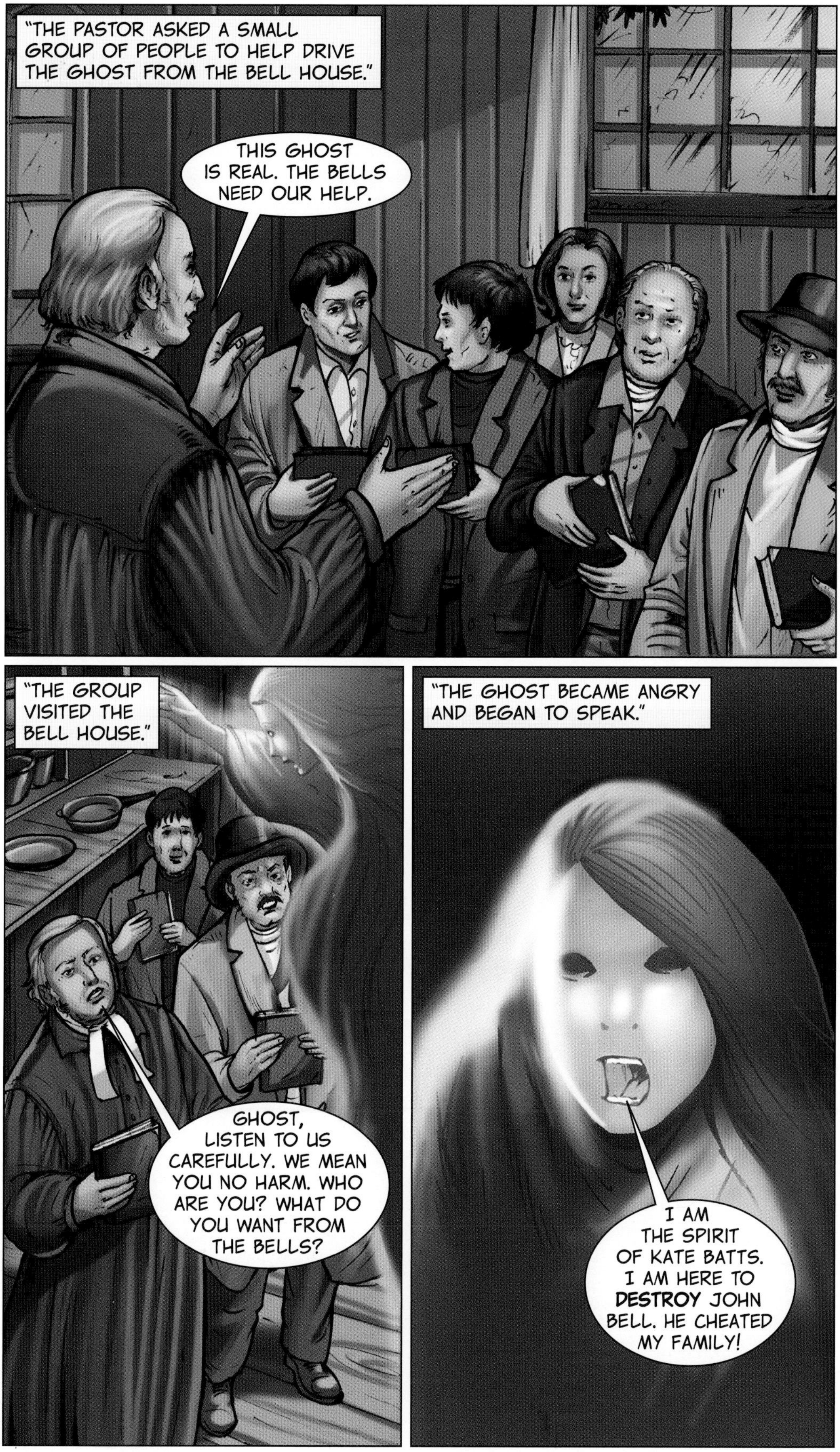
"THE PASTOR ASKED A SMALL GROUP OF PEOPLE TO HELP DRIVE THE GHOST FROM THE BELL HOUSE."
THIS GHOST IS REAL. THE BELLS NEED OUR HELP.
"THE GROUP VISITED THE BELL HOUSE."
GHOST, LISTEN TO US CAREFULLY. WE MEAN YOU NO HARM. WHO ARE YOU? WHAT DO YOU WANT FROM THE BELLS?
"THE GHOST BECAME ANGRY AND BEGAN TO SPEAK."
I AM THE SPIRIT OF KATE BATTS. I AM HERE TO **DESTROY** JOHN BELL. HE CHEATED MY FAMILY!

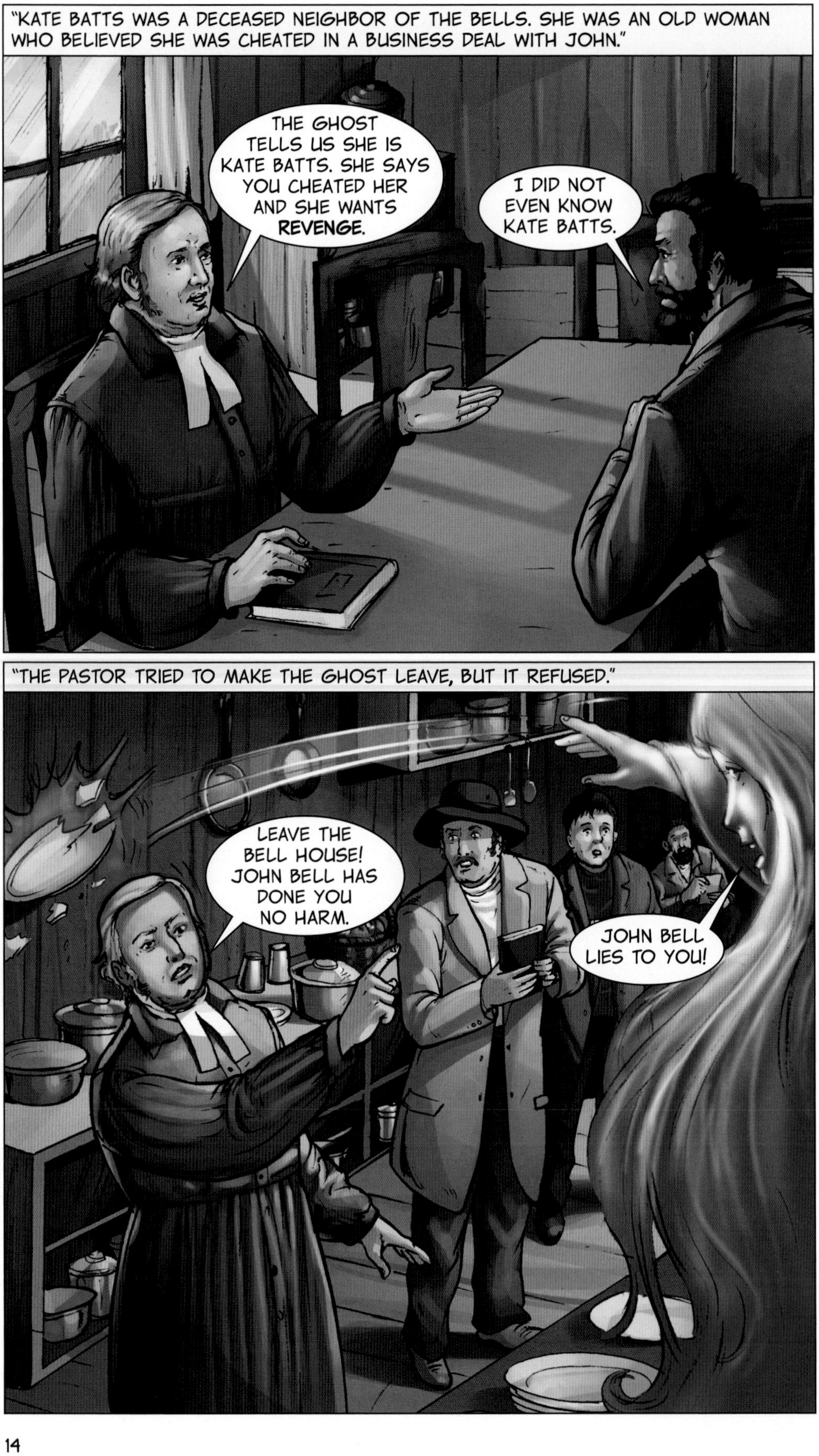
"KATE BATTS WAS A DECEASED NEIGHBOR OF THE BELLS. SHE WAS AN OLD WOMAN WHO BELIEVED SHE WAS CHEATED IN A BUSINESS DEAL WITH JOHN."
THE GHOST TELLS US SHE IS KATE BATTS. SHE SAYS YOU CHEATED HER AND SHE WANTS **REVENGE**.
I DID NOT EVEN KNOW KATE BATTS.
"THE PASTOR TRIED TO MAKE THE GHOST LEAVE, BUT IT REFUSED."
LEAVE THE BELL HOUSE! JOHN BELL HAS DONE YOU NO HARM.
JOHN BELL LIES TO YOU!

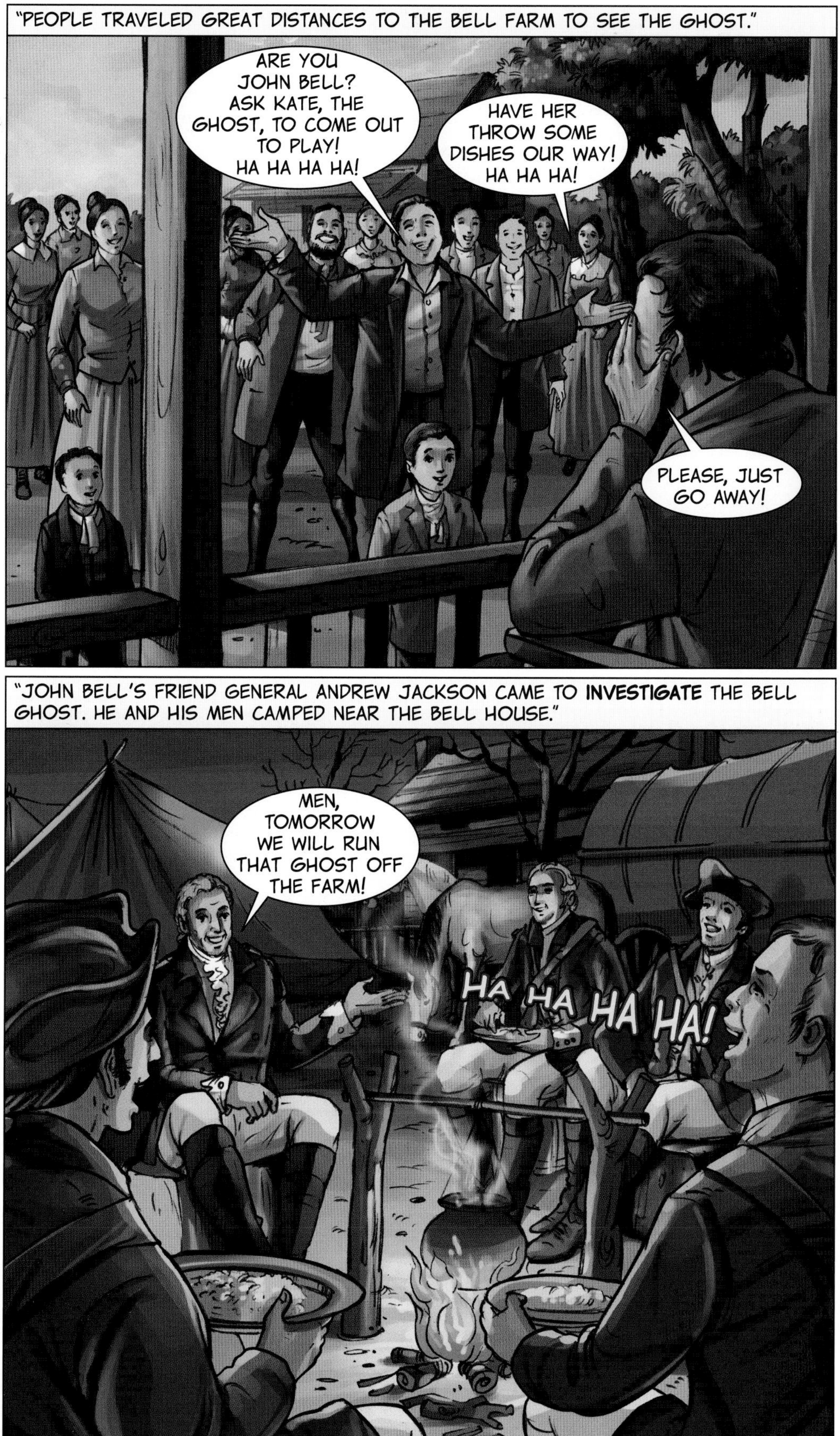
"PEOPLE TRAVELED GREAT DISTANCES TO THE BELL FARM TO SEE THE GHOST."
ARE YOU JOHN BELL? ASK KATE, THE GHOST, TO COME OUT TO PLAY! HA HA HA HA!
HAVE HER THROW SOME DISHES OUR WAY! HA HA HA!
PLEASE, JUST GO AWAY!
"JOHN BELL'S FRIEND GENERAL ANDREW JACKSON CAME TO **INVESTIGATE** THE BELL GHOST. HE AND HIS MEN CAMPED NEAR THE BELL HOUSE."
MEN, TOMORROW WE WILL RUN THAT GHOST OFF THE FARM!
HA HA HA HA!

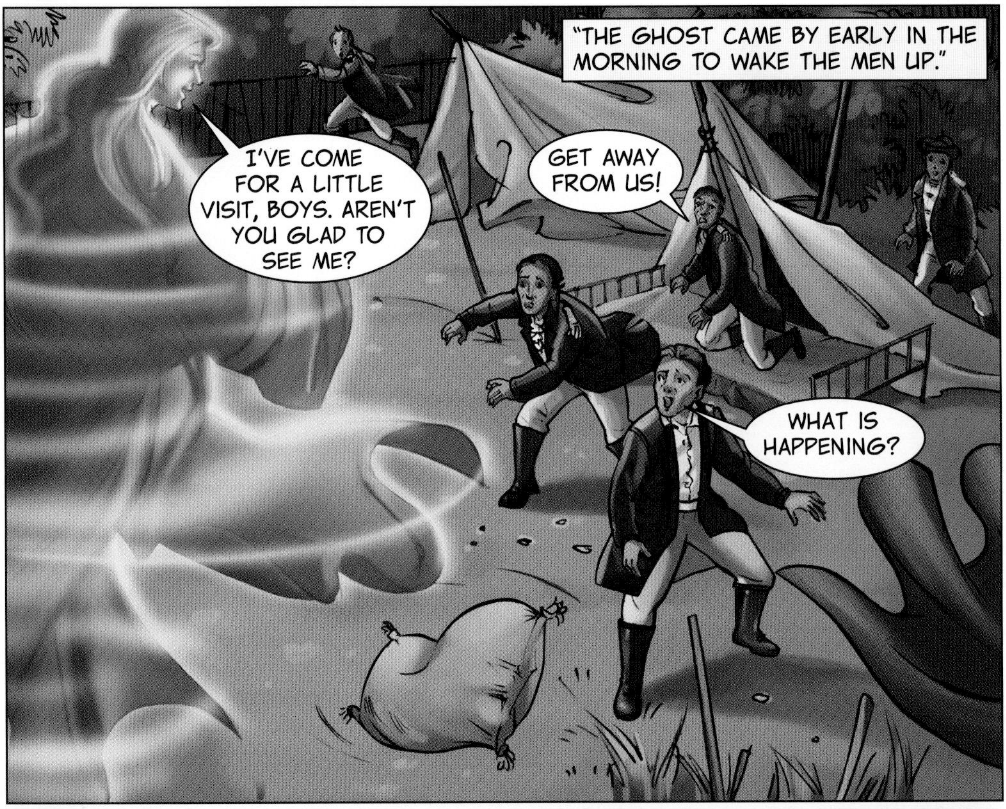
"THE GHOST CAME BY EARLY IN THE MORNING TO WAKE THE MEN UP."
I'VE COME FOR A LITTLE VISIT, BOYS. AREN'T YOU GLAD TO SEE ME?
GET AWAY FROM US!
WHAT IS HAPPENING?

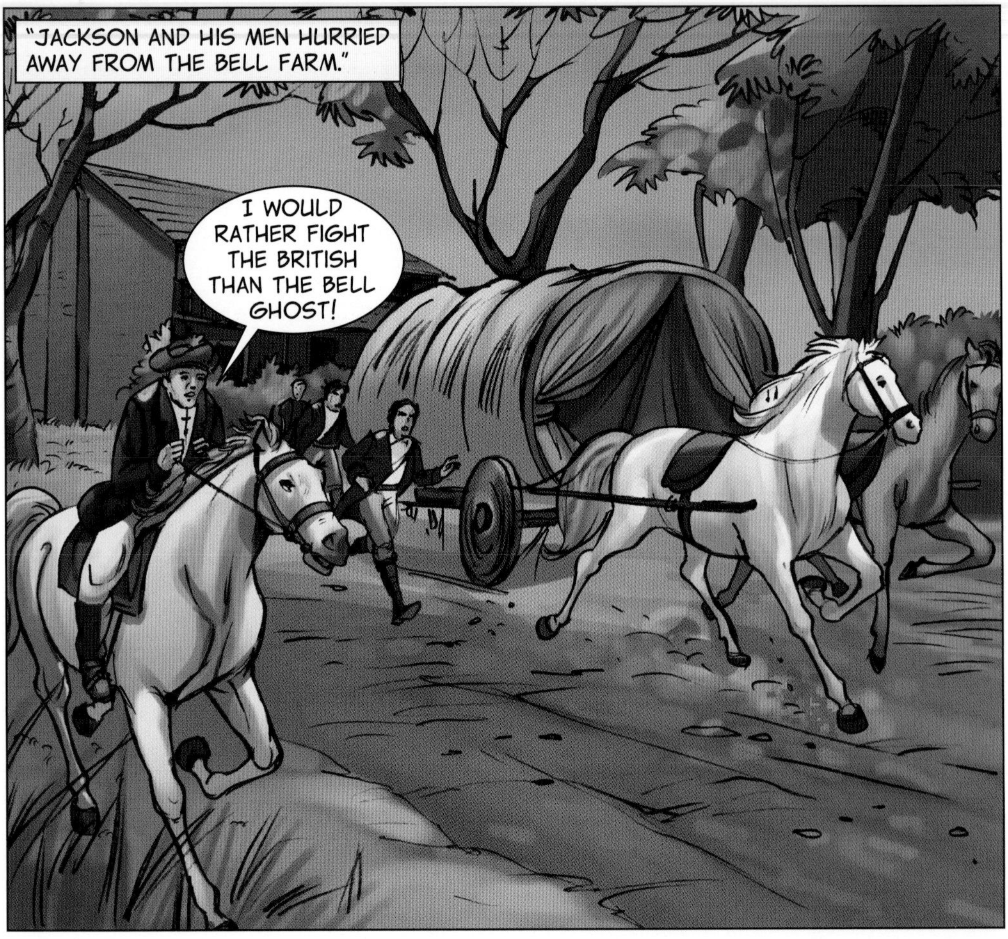
"JACKSON AND HIS MEN HURRIED AWAY FROM THE BELL FARM."
I WOULD RATHER FIGHT THE BRITISH THAN THE BELL GHOST!

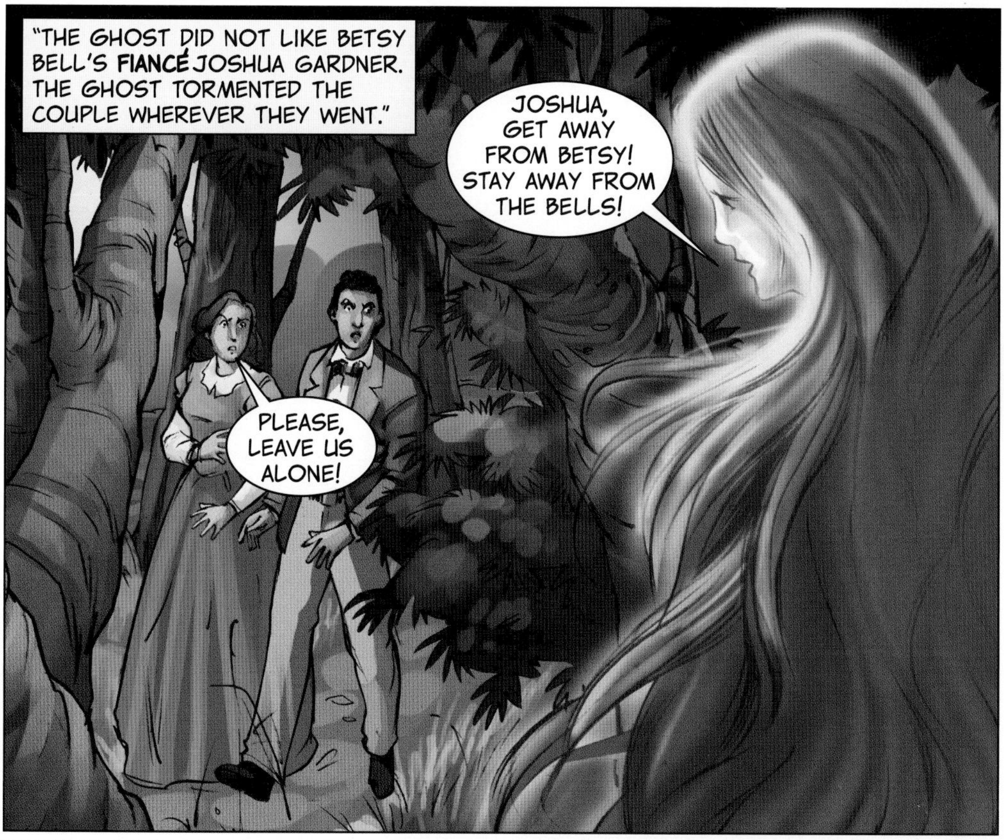
"THE GHOST DID NOT LIKE BETSY BELL'S **FIANCÉ** JOSHUA GARDNER. THE GHOST TORMENTED THE COUPLE WHEREVER THEY WENT."
JOSHUA, GET AWAY FROM BETSY! STAY AWAY FROM THE BELLS!
PLEASE, LEAVE US ALONE!

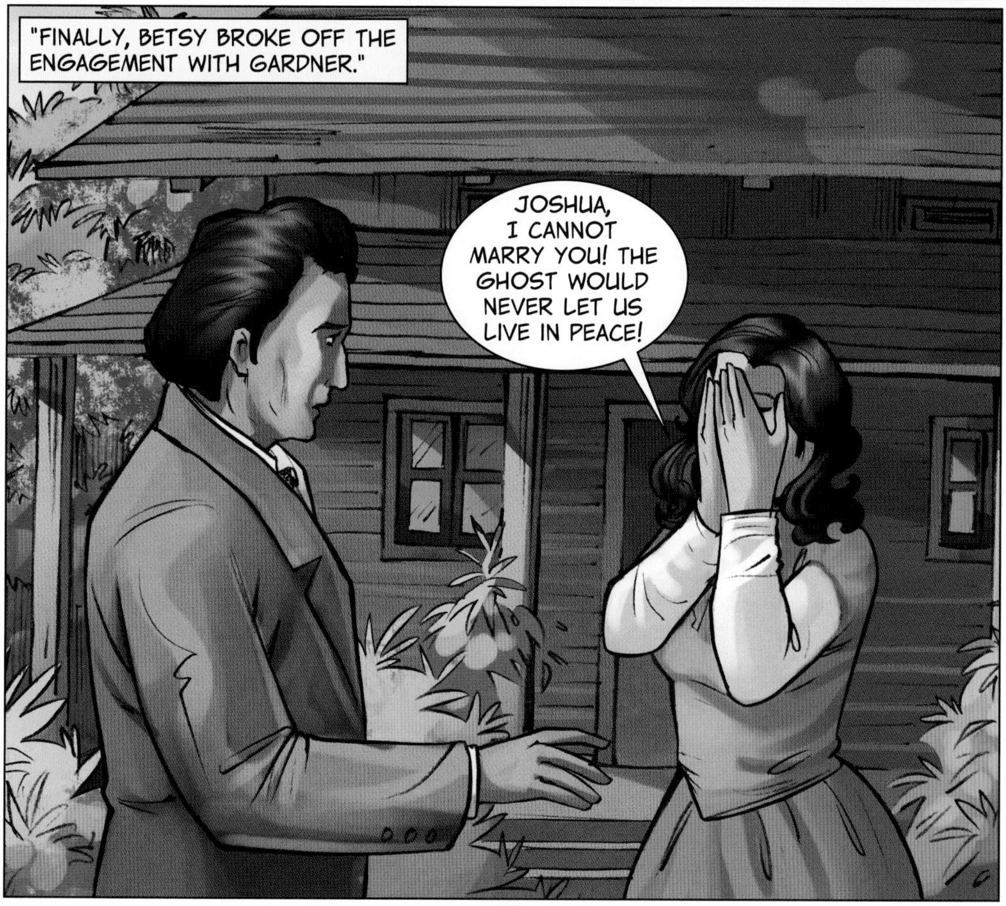
"FINALLY, BETSY BROKE OFF THE ENGAGEMENT WITH GARDNER."
JOSHUA, I CANNOT MARRY YOU! THE GHOST WOULD NEVER LET US LIVE IN PEACE!

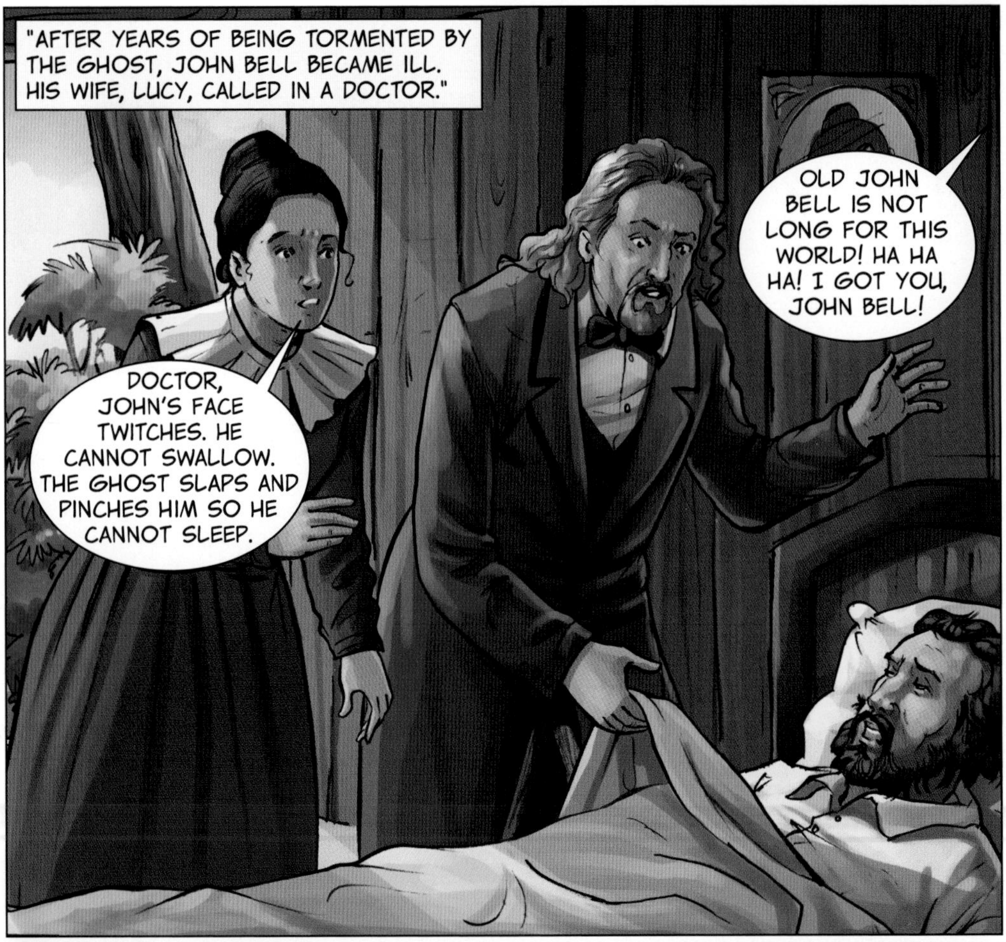
"AFTER YEARS OF BEING TORMENTED BY THE GHOST, JOHN BELL BECAME ILL. HIS WIFE, LUCY, CALLED IN A DOCTOR."
DOCTOR, JOHN'S FACE TWITCHES. HE CANNOT SWALLOW. THE GHOST SLAPS AND PINCHES HIM SO HE CANNOT SLEEP.
OLD JOHN BELL IS NOT LONG FOR THIS WORLD! HA HA HA! I GOT YOU, JOHN BELL!

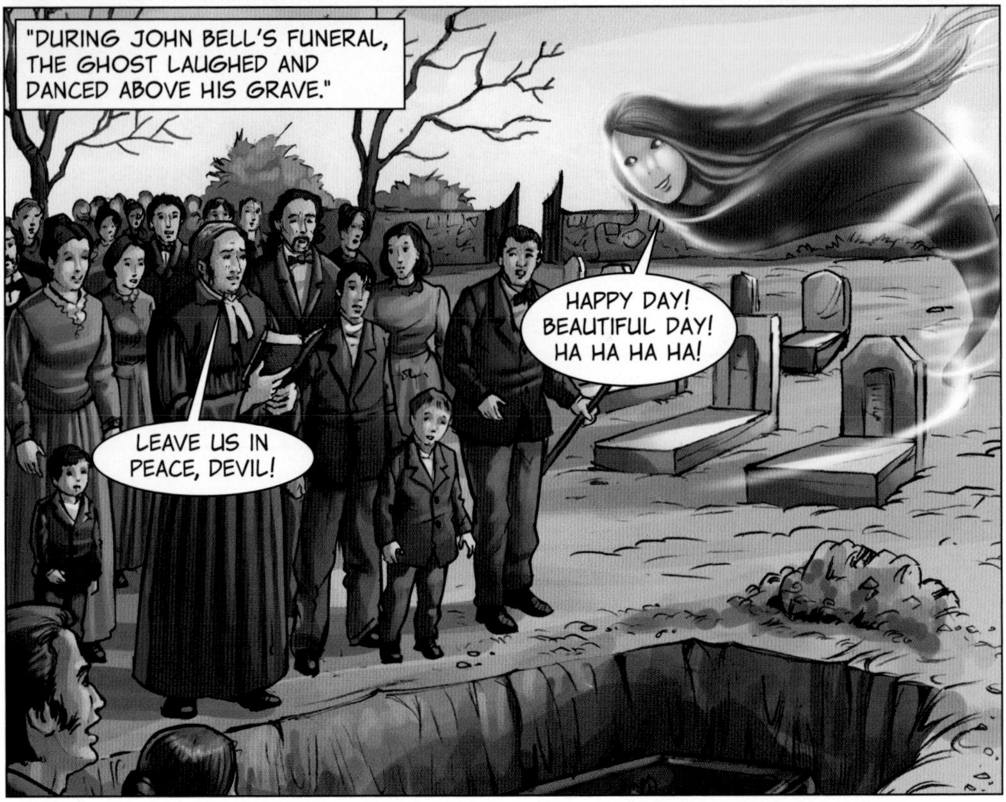
"DURING JOHN BELL'S FUNERAL, THE GHOST LAUGHED AND DANCED ABOVE HIS GRAVE."
HAPPY DAY! BEAUTIFUL DAY! HA HA HA HA!
LEAVE US IN PEACE, DEVIL!

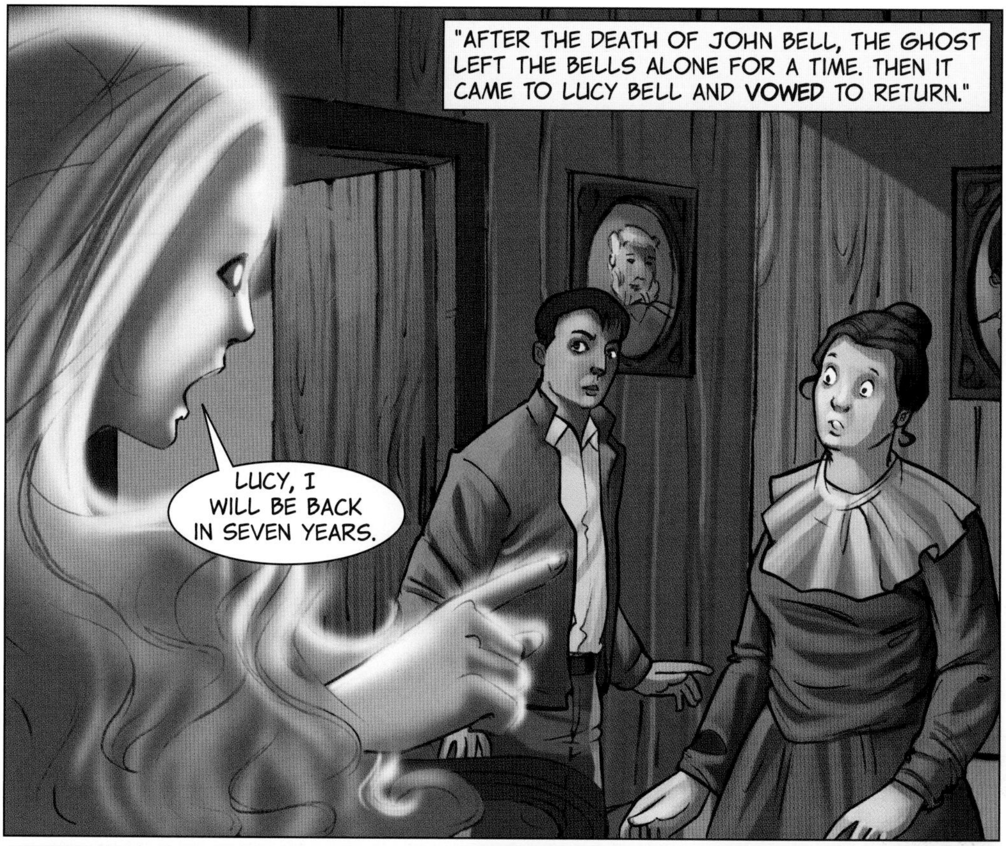
"AFTER THE DEATH OF JOHN BELL, THE GHOST LEFT THE BELLS ALONE FOR A TIME. THEN IT CAME TO LUCY BELL AND **VOWED** TO RETURN."
LUCY, I WILL BE BACK IN SEVEN YEARS.

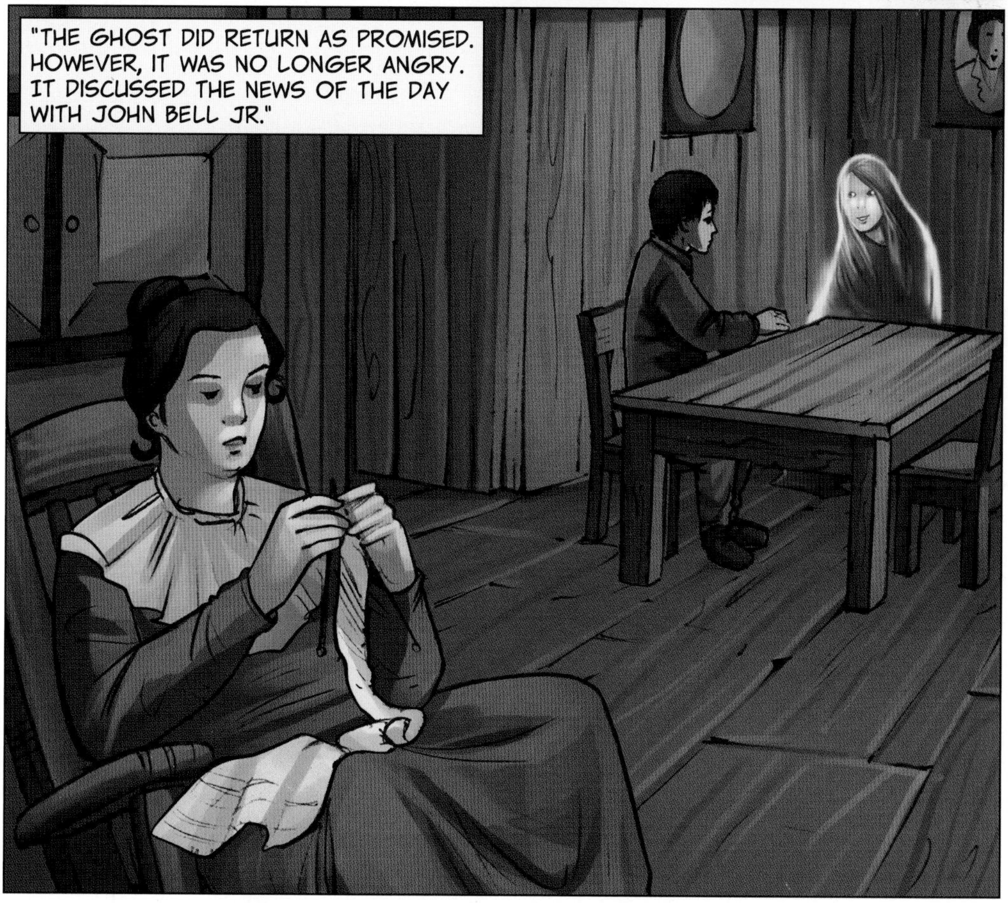
"THE GHOST DID RETURN AS PROMISED. HOWEVER, IT WAS NO LONGER ANGRY. IT DISCUSSED THE NEWS OF THE DAY WITH JOHN BELL JR."

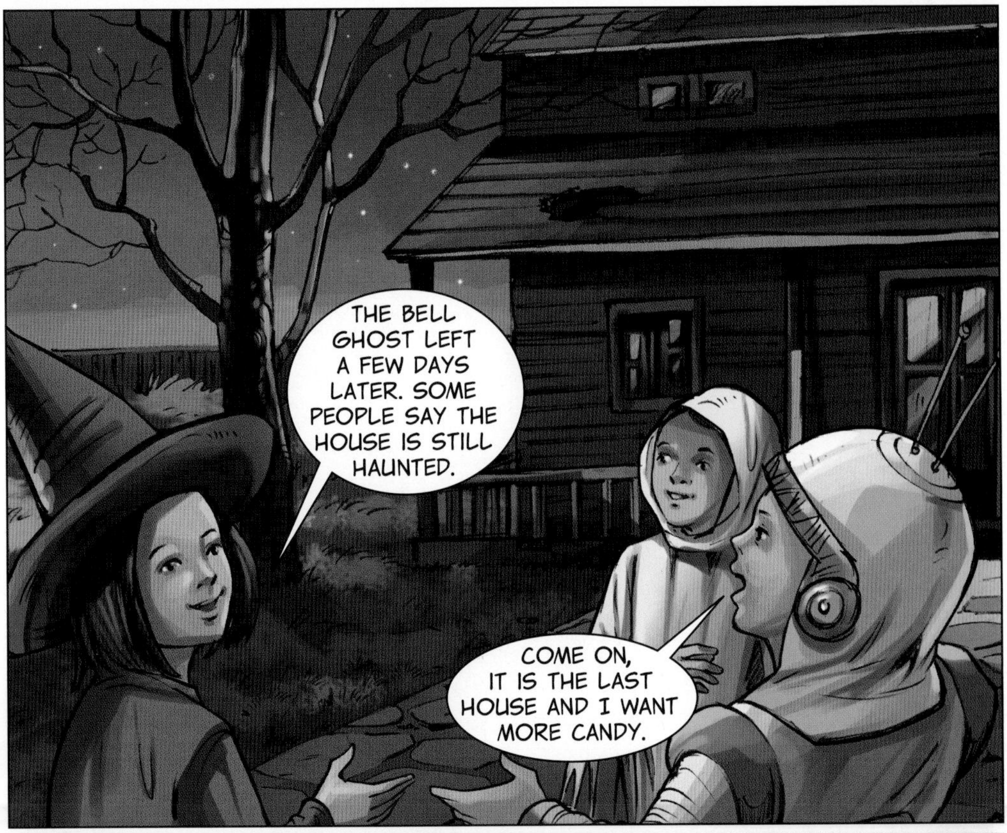
THE BELL GHOST LEFT A FEW DAYS LATER. SOME PEOPLE SAY THE HOUSE IS STILL HAUNTED.
COME ON, IT IS THE LAST HOUSE AND I WANT MORE CANDY.

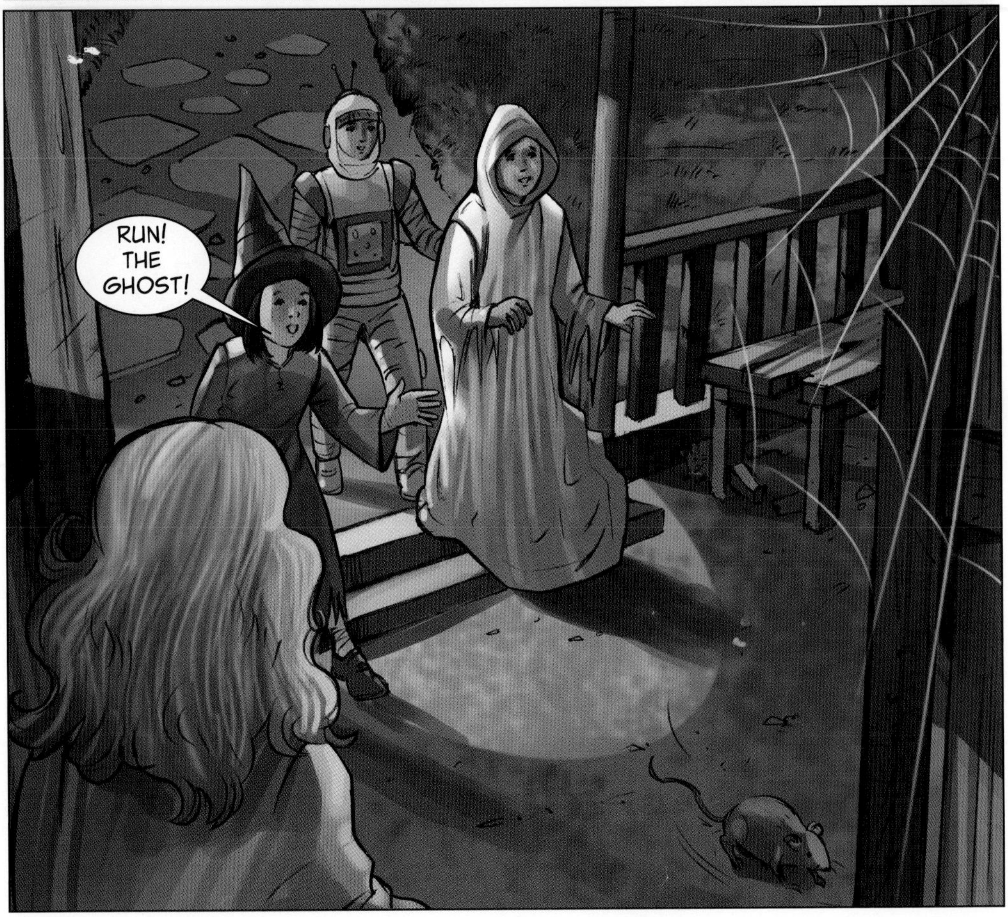
RUN! THE GHOST!

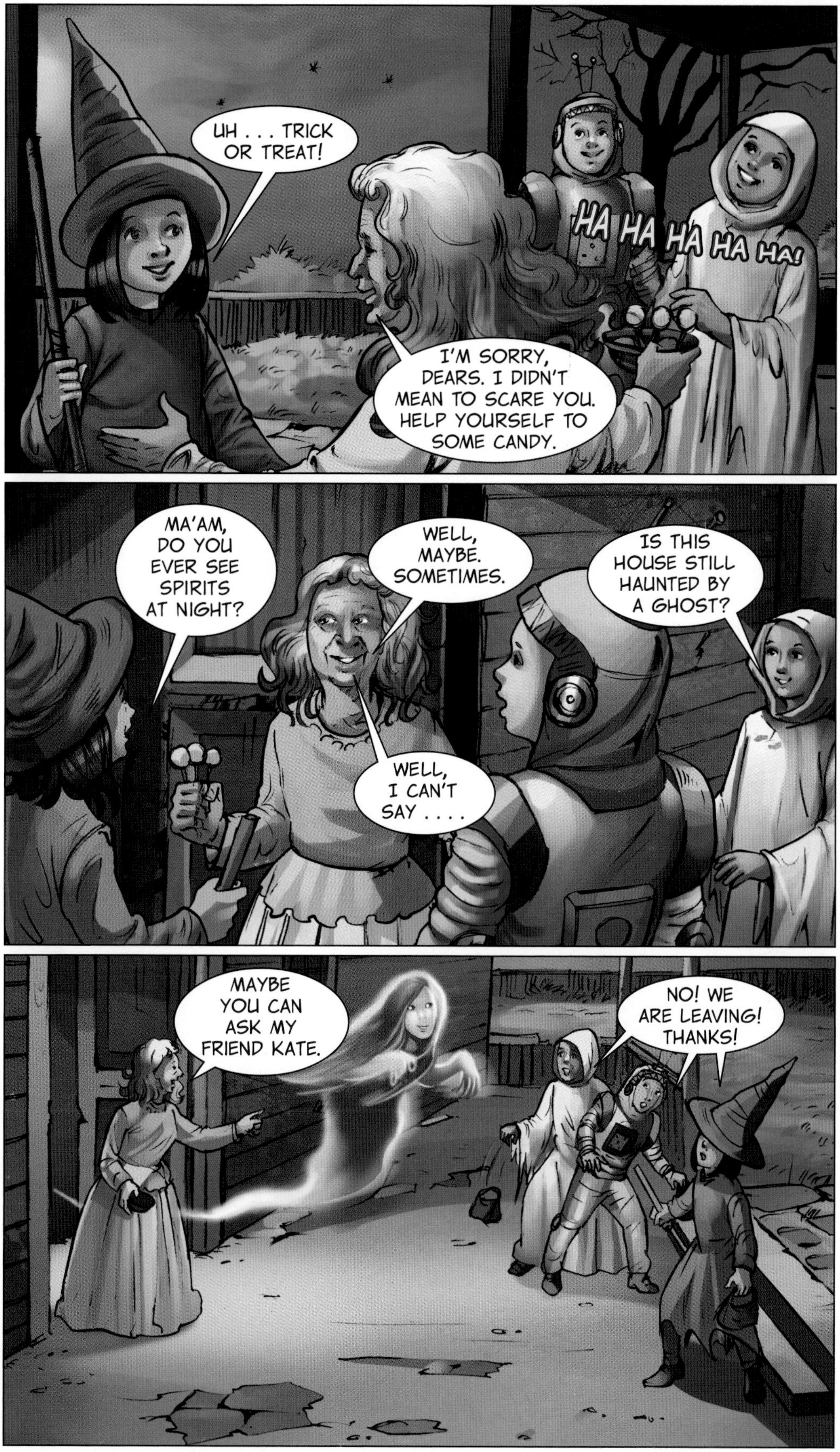
UH . . . TRICK OR TREAT!
HA HA HA HA HA!
I'M SORRY, DEARS. I DIDN'T MEAN TO SCARE YOU. HELP YOURSELF TO SOME CANDY.
MA'AM, DO YOU EVER SEE SPIRITS AT NIGHT?
WELL, MAYBE. SOMETIMES.
IS THIS HOUSE STILL HAUNTED BY A GHOST?
WELL, I CAN'T SAY . . . .
MAYBE YOU CAN ASK MY FRIEND KATE.
NO! WE ARE LEAVING! THANKS!

More Ghost Stories

- **Famous Ghosts** Some people think that the ghost of Benjamin Franklin haunts the American Philosophical Society building in Philadelphia, Pennsylvania. His spirit has been seen dancing nearby in the street. It has been said that the ghosts of Abraham Lincoln and Franklin D. Roosevelt haunt the White House in Washington, D.C.

- **Haunted Hotel** The Ivy House Inn in Casper, Wyoming, was bought by Tom and Kathy Johnson in 1995 after the death of the previous owner, Mrs. White. The ghost of Mrs. White did not like some of Tom Johnson's **remodeling**. Some of Tom's power tools suddenly stopped working. Tools flew through the air and out of the room. Guests sometimes hear and see the spirits of Mrs. White's dead cats at different places in the hotel.

- **Ghosts in Salem, Massachusetts** During the Salem witch trials in the late 1600s, accused witches were held in terrible conditions in small jail cells. These cells became known as the witch **dungeon**. Today the old jail has been remodeled. The building has condominiums, a restaurant, and a museum. Some think that the spirits of those who were jailed there haunt the building. People have reported hearing strange sounds and seeing ghosts that walk through walls.

Glossary

cheated (CHEETD) Acted dishonestly.

deceased (dih-SEESD) Dead.

destroy (dih-STROY) To tear apart or ruin.

dungeon (DUN-jen) A dark, often underground prison.

engagement (in-GAYJ-ment) A promise to marry.

experts (EK-sperts) People who know a lot about a subject.

fiancé (fee-ahn-SAY) A man who has promised to marry someone.

haunt (HAWNT) To be visited by a ghost.

investigate (in-VES-tuh-gayt) To try to learn the facts about something.

remodeling (ree-MO-del-ing) Changing parts of a building.

revenge (rih-VENJ) Hurting someone in return for hurting you.

spirit (SPIR-ut) The ghost or soul of a dead person.

tormented (tawr-MENT-ed) Caused someone great pain of the mind or body.

vowed (VOWD) Made a very important promise.

Index

Web Sites

Due to the changing nature of Internet links, PowerKids Press has developed an online list of Web sites related to the subject of this book. This site is updated regularly. Please use this link to access the list:

www.powerkidslinks.com/mons/ghosts/